CONTENTS

CAP sleeve pullover

Rose Callahan

You'll Need

YARN (1)

- 3½oz/100g, 360yd/330m (3½oz/100g, 360yd/330m; 5¼oz/150g, 540yd/500m; 5¼oz/150g, 540yd/500m; 7oz/200g, 720yd/660m; 7oz/200g, 720yd/660m; 8¾oz/250g, 900yd/825m) of any fingering weight cotton in yellow (MC) and cream (CC)

NEEDLES

- One pair size 6 (4mm) knitting needles *or size to obtain gauge.*

OTHER MATERIALS

- One size D-3 (3.25mm) crochet hook
- Stitch holder

SIZES

Sized for X-Small, Small, Medium, Large, 1X, 2X, 3X. Shown in size Small.

KNITTED MEASUREMENTS

- **Bust** 28 (32, 36, 40, 44, 48, 52)"/71 (81, 91.5, 101.5, 111.5, 122, 132)cm
- **Length** 15 (15½, 16½, 17½, 18½, 20½, 21½)"/38 (39.5, 41.5, 44.5, 47, 52, 54.5)cm

GAUGE

20 sts and 20 rows to 4"/10cm over garter st using size 6 (4mm) needles. *Take time to check gauge.*

STITCH GLOSSARY

Stripe pattern
*2 rows MC, 2 rows CC; rep from * (4 rows) for stripe pat.

BACK

With MC, cast on 72 (82, 92, 102, 112, 122, 132) sts. Work in garter st (knit every row) and stripe pat as foll:

For sizes XS, S, M, L only
Work as established until piece measures 15 (15½, 16½, 17½)"/38 (39.5, 41.5, 44.5)cm from beg. Bind off all sts.

For sizes 1X, 2X, 3X only
Work as established until piece measures (10½, 12, 12½)"/(26.5, 30.5, 31.5)cm from beg.

Shape armhole
Dec 1 st each side on next row, then every other row twice more—(106, 116, 126) sts. Work even until piece measures (18½, 20½, 21½)"/(47, 52, 54.5)cm from beg.
Bind off all sts.

FRONT

Work same as back until piece measures 8½ (8½, 9, 9½, 10, 11½, 12)"/21.5 (21.5, 23, 24, 25.5, 29, 30.5)cm from beg.

Separate for neck
Next row (RS) K36 (41, 46, 51, 53, 58, 63) slip these sts just worked to holder for left front, k36 (41, 46, 51, 53, 58, 63). Cont working in garter st stripe pat as established on these sts until right front measures same as back. Bind off. Slip sts from left front holder and complete as for right front.

FINISHING

Sew bound-off edges together, leaving 6 (6, 6½, 7, 7, 7½, 7½)"/15 (15, 16.5, 18, 18, 19, 19)cm open at center for neck. Sew side seams, leaving 6 (6½, 7, 7½, 8, 8½, 9)"/15 (16.5, 17.5, 19, 20.5, 21.5, 23)cm open to the shoulder for armholes.
With crochet hook and MC, work a single round of backwards sc (from right to left) around neck and armhole openings.

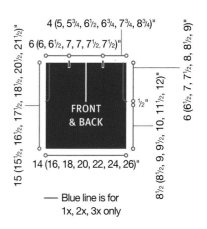

4 (5, 5¾, 6½, 6¾, 7¾, 8¾)"

6 (6, 6½, 7, 7, 7½, 7½)"

15 (15½, 16½, 17½, 18½, 20½, 21½)"

FRONT & BACK

½"

6 (6½, 7, 7½, 8, 8½, 9)"

14 (16, 18, 20, 22, 24, 26)"

8½ (8½, 9, 9½, 10, 11½, 12)"

— Blue line is for 1x, 2x, 3x only

BUTTON banded v-neck top

You'll Need

YARN 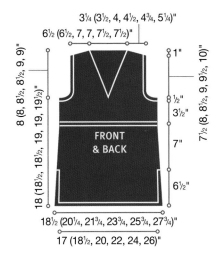 3

- 12oz/325g, 750yd/685m (14oz/390g, 900yd/820m; 14oz/390g, 900yd/820m; 16oz/450g, 1050yd/960m; 16oz/450g, 1050yd/960m; 19oz/520g, 1200yd/1100m; 21oz/590g, 1350yd/1240m) of any DK weight cotton

NEEDLES

- One size 6 (4mm) circular needle, 32"/80cm long *or size to obtain gauge.*
- One size 6 (4mm) circular needle, 16"/40cm long

OTHER MATERIALS

- 4 stitch markers
- Scrap yarn or stitch holders
- Assorted novelty buttons

SIZES

Sized for Small, Medium, Large, 1X, 2X, 3X. Shown in size Small.

KNITTED MEASUREMENTS

- **Bust** 34 (37, 40, 44, 48, 52)"/86.5 (94, 101.5, 111.5, 122,132)cm
- **Length** 26 (26½, 27, 27½, 28, 28½)"/66 (67.5, 68.5, 70, 71, 72.5) cm

GAUGE

20 sts and 28 rows to 4"/10cm over St st using size 5 (3.75mm) needles. *Take time to check gauge.*

STITCH GLOSSARY

Seed stitch
(multiple of 2 sts plus 1)
Row 1 (RS) K1, *p1, k1 from * to end.
Row 2 Knit the p sts and purl the k sts.
Rep row 2 for seed st.

BACK

Cast on 93 (101, 109, 119, 129, 139) sts. Work in seed st for 4 rows.

Side slits
Next row (RS) Work in seed st across first 2 (2, 2, 4, 4, 4) sts, pm, k to last 2 (2, 2, 4, 4, 4) sts, pm, work in seed st across last 2 (2, 2, 4, 4, 4) sts. Keeping 2 (2, 2, 4, 4, 4) sts each side in seed st, and rem sts in St st, work even until piece measures 2½"/6.5cm from beg, end with a WS row.

Shape sides
Next (dec) row (RS) Work in seed st to first marker, sl marker, k2tog, work to 2 sts before next marker, ssk, sl marker, work in seed st to end. Rep dec row every 18th row 4 times more. AT THE SAME TIME, when piece measures 6½"/16.5cm from beg, end with a WS row. Cast on 1 st at beg of next 2 rows, dropping markers on last row. Cont in St st on all sts. When all shaping has been completed, work even on 85 (93, 101, 111, 121, 131) sts until piece measures 13½"/34cm from beg, end with a WS row. Work in seed st for 2 rows for seed st band. Cont in St st until piece measures 17"/43cm from beg, end with a WS row.
Next row (RS) Work in seed st across first 7 (8, 9, 11, 12, 13) sts, pm, k to end.
Next row Work in seed st across first 7 (8, 9, 11, 12, 13) sts, pm, p to marker, sl marker, work in seed st across last 7 (8, 9, 11, 12, 13) sts to end. Keeping 7 (8, 9, 11, 12, 13) sts each side in seed st and rem sts in St st, work even for 0 (0, 0, 2, 2, 2) rows.

3¼ (3½, 4, 4½, 4¾, 5¼)"
6½ (6½, 7, 7, 7½, 7½)"
8 (8, 8½, 8½, 9, 9)"
1"
½"
3½"
7½ (8, 8½, 9, 9½, 10)"
FRONT & BACK
7"
6½"
18 (18½, 18½, 19, 19, 19½)"
18½ (20¼, 21¾, 23¾, 25¾, 27¾)"
17 (18½, 20, 22, 24, 26)"

Rose Callahan

Shape armholes

Bind off 5 (6, 7, 7, 8, 9) sts in seed st at beg of next 2 rows.

Next (dec) row (RS) Work in seed st to first marker, sl marker, k2tog, work to 2 sts before next marker, ssk, sl marker, work in seed st to end. Rep dec row every other row 4 (5, 5, 7, 9, 11) times more—65 (69, 75, 81, 85, 89) sts. Work even until armhole measures 7½ (8, 8½, 9, 9½, 10)"/19 (20.5, 21.5, 23, 24, 25.5)cm, end with a WS row dropping markers.

Shape shoulders

Bind off 5 (6, 7, 8, 8, 9) sts at beg of next 4 rows, then 6 (6, 6, 7, 8, 8) sts at beg of next 2 rows. Bind off rem 33 (33, 35, 35, 37, 37) sts for back neck.

FRONT

Work same as back until armhole measures 1 (1½, 1½, 2, 2, 2½)"/2.5 (4, 4, 5, 5, 6.5)cm, end with a WS row.

Shape neck

Cont to shape armholes, work as foll:

Next row (RS) Work across to center st, place center st on holder, join a 2nd ball of yarn, work to end. Working both sides at once, work next row even. Dec 1 st from each neck edge on next row, then every other row 15 (15, 16, 16, 17, 17) times more. Work even on 16 (18, 20, 23, 24, 26) sts each side until piece measures same length as back to shoulder, end with a WS row. Shape shoulders same as back.

FINISHING

Block pieces to measurements. Sew shoulder seams.

Neckband

With RS facing and circular needle, beg at right shoulder seam, pick up and k 29 (29, 31, 31, 33, 33) sts evenly spaced along back neck edge, 42 (42, 44, 44, 46, 46) sts along left neck edge, pm, p 1 st from holder, pm, pick up and k 42 (42, 44, 44, 46, 46) sts evenly spaced along left neck edge—113 (113, 119, 119, 125, 125) sts. Join and pm for beg of rnds. **Rnd 1 (RS)** K1, *p1, k1; rep from * to 2 sts before first marker, p2tog, sl marker, k1, p2tog tbl, *k1, p1; rep from * to end. **Rnd 2** P1, *k1, p1; rep from * to 2 sts before first marker, p2tog, sl marker, p1, sl marker, p2tog tbl, *p1, k1; rep from * to end. **Rnd 3** Rep rnd 1.

For sizes 1X, 2X and 3X only

Rep rnd 2.

For all sizes

Bind off loosely in seed st. Sew side seams to top of side slits. Sew buttons on top of seed st band; as shown.

RUCHED tank top

You'll Need

YARN (3)

- 7oz/200g, 600yd/530m (8¾oz/250g, 730yd/660m; 10½oz/300g, 880yd/800m; 10½oz/300g, 880yd/800m; 12¼oz/350g, 1030yd/930m; 14oz/400g, 1170yd/1070m) of any DK weight wool blend.

NEEDLES

- One pair size 5 (3.75mm) needles *or size to obtain gauge.*
- One size 5 (3.75mm) circular needle, 24"/60cm long

OTHER MATERIALS

- Two size 5 (3.75mm) double-pointed needles
- Two split stitch markers

SIZES

Sized for Small, Medium, Large, 1X, 2X, 3X. Shown in size Small.

KNITTED MEASUREMENTS

- **Bust** 32 (36, 40, 44, 48, 52)"/81 (91.5, 101.5, 111.5, 122, 132cm
- **Length** 21 (21½, 22, 22½, 23, 23½)"/53.5 (54.5, 56, 57, 58.5, 59.5 cm

NOTE

Schematic reflects length before neck and armhole finishing.

GAUGE

24 sts and 28 rows to 4"/10cm over St st using size 5 (3.75mm) needles.
Take time to check gauge.

BACK

With size 5 (3.75mm) needles, cast on 96 (108, 120, 132, 144, 156) sts. Work in St st (k on RS, p on WS) until piece measures 3"/7.5cm from beg, end with a WS row.

Shape waist
Next (dec) row (RS) K1, ssk, k to last 3 sts, k2tog, k1—94 (106, 118, 130, 142, 154) sts.
Rep dec row every 8th row twice more, then every 6th row twice—86 (98, 110, 122, 134, 146) sts. Work even until piece measures 10"/25.5cm from beg, end with a WS row.
Next (inc) row (RS) K1, inc 1 into next st, k to last 2 sts, inc 1 into next st, k1.
Rep inc row every 6th row once more, then every 4th row 3 times—96 (108, 120, 132, 144, 156) sts.
Work even in St st until piece measures 14"/35.5cm from beg, end with WS row.

Shape armhole
Bind off 4 (5, 6, 6, 6, 6) sts at beg of next 2 (2, 2, 2, 2, 4) rows, then 2 (2, 2, 4, 4, 4) sts at beg of next 2 (2, 4, 4, 6, 6) rows. Dec 1 st each side every other row 3 (3, 3, 5, 6, 6) times—78 (88, 94, 94, 96, 96) sts. Work even until armhole measures 7 (7½, 8, 8½, 9, 9½)"/18 (19, 20.5, 21.5, 23, 24)cm, end with a WS row.
Next row K19 (23, 25, 25, 25, 25), join 2nd ball of yarn, bind off center 40 (42, 44, 44, 46, 46) sts, k to end.
Working both sides at once, dec 1 st at neck edge every other row 3 times—16 (20, 22, 22, 22, 22) sts rem for each shoulder.
Work even until armhole measures 9 (9½, 10, 10½, 11, 11½)"/23 (24, 25.5, 26.5, 28, 29)cm. Bind off.

FRONT

Work same as for back until all armhole shaping is complete—78 (88, 94, 96, 96) sts. Beg neck shaping as foll:
Next row (RS) K39 (44, 47, 47, 48, 48), turn work. Working these 39 (44, 47, 47, 48, 48) sts only for left front, work 4 rows even.

Shape neck
Next row (WS) Bind off 2 sts, p to end. Bind off 2 sts at neck edge every 4th row 5 times more, bind off 4 sts every 4th row at neck edge twice. Place marker in last bound-off st. P2tog at neck edge every WS row 3 (4, 5, 5, 6, 6) times—16 (20, 22, 22, 22, 22) sts rem for shoulder. Work even until armhole measures same as back. Bind off.
Rejoin yarn at center to work right front beg with a WS row. Work same as for left front reversing shaping by working neck edge bind-offs on RS rows and decs as ssk on RS rows.

FINISHING

Sew shoulder and side seams.

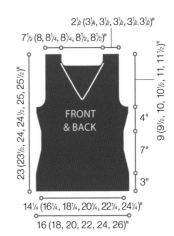

Rose Callahan

Neck edging

With circular needle, beg at left shoulder seam, pick up and k 1 st in each st to marker. *Pick up and k 1 st in the last bound-off st, pick up and k 1 st in first bound off st, skipping all sts in between; rep from * to center of front neck, pick up and k 1 st at center, cont to pick up and k sts in same manner to marker, then pick up and k 1 st in each st along rem neck edge. Cut yarn, leaving long tail.

I-cord bind-off

Bind off all sts using applied I-cord as foll: With dpns, cast on 3 sts. *K2, k next st tog tbl with the next st on circular needle. Without turning work, slide the 3 sts back to beg of the row. Pull yarn tightly from the end of the row. Rep from * until all sts from circular needle have been worked. Bind off 3 sts. Sew ends of I-cord tog.

Armhole edging

With circular needle, pick up and k 100 (108, 116, 122, 130, 136) sts evenly spaced along armhole edge. **Note** It will be necessary to skip rows in order to pick up the correct number of sts to slightly pucker the armhole edge. Work I-cord bind-off same as for neck.

STRIPED tank

Rose Callahan

You'll Need

YARN (4)

- 3½oz/100g, 300yd/270m (3½oz/100g, 300yd/270m; 5oz/140g, 400yd/360m; 5oz/140g, 400yd/360m; 6oz/170g, 500yd/450m; 7¼oz/200g, 600yd/540m) of any worsted weight cotton in yellow (A)
- 2½oz/70g, 200yd/180m (2½oz/70g, 200yd/180m; 3½oz/100g, 300yd/270m; 3½oz/100g, 300yd/270m; 3½oz/100g, 300yd/270m; 5oz/140g, 400yd/360m) in orange (B)

NEEDLES

- 1 pair each sizes 6 and 8 (4 and 5mm) needles *or size to obtain gauge.*

OTHER MATERIALS

- Stitch markers
- Tapestry needle

SIZES

Sized for X-Small (Small, Medium, Large, 1X, 2X). Shown in size X-Small.

KNITTED MEASUREMENTS

- **Bust** 30 (34, 38, 42, 46, 50)"/76 (84.5, 96.5, 106.5, 117, 127)cm
- **Length (including straps)** 17½ (18, 19, 19½, 20½, 21)"/44.5 (45.5, 48.5, 49.5, 52, 53.5)cm

GAUGE

20 sts and 26 rows to 4"/10cm over St st using larger needles.
Take time to check gauge.

STRIPE PATTERN

8 rows A, 2 rows B.
Rep these 10 rows for stripe pat.

BACK

With smaller needles and B, cast on 75 (85, 95, 105, 115, 125). Work in k1, p1 rib for 6 rows. Change to larger needles and work in St st and stripe pat for 10 rows.
Next (dec) row (RS) K1, ssk, k to last 3 sts, k2tog, k1. Rep dec row every 4th row 3 times more—67 (77, 87, 97, 107, 117) sts. Work even until piece measures 7 (7, 7½, 7½, 8, 8)"/18 (18, 19, 19, 20.5, 20.5) cm from beg, ending with a WS row.
Next (inc) row (RS) K1, M1, k to last st, M1, k1. Rep inc row every 6th row 3 times more—75 (85, 95, 105, 115, 125). Work even until piece measures 10½ (10½, 11, 11, 11½, 11½)"/26.5 (26.5, 28, 28, 29, 29)cm, ending with a WS row.

Armhole shaping

Next (RS) row Cont in stripe pat, k1, [k1, p1] twice, ssk, k to last 7 sts, k2tog, [p1, k1] twice, k1.
Next (WS) row P1, [p1, k1] twice, p2tog, p to last 7 sts, p2tog tbl, [k1, p1] twice, p1.
Rep last 2 rows 3 times more—59 (69, 79, 89, 99, 109) sts.**

[continued]

Next (RS) row Change to smaller needles and B, k1 [k1, p1] twice, ssk, work in p1, k1 rib to last 8 sts, p1, k2tog, [p1, k1] twice, k1—57 (67, 77, 87, 97, 107) sts. Work in rib as established for 3 rows. Bind off.

FRONT

Work as for back to **—59 (69, 79, 89, 99, 109) sts.

Neck shaping

Dec row 1 (RS) K1, [k1, p1] twice, ssk, k 19 (24, 29, 34, 39, 44) sts, k2tog, k1, place next st on holder, attach a second ball of yarn, k1, ssk, k 19 (24, 29, 34, 39, 44) sts, k2tog, [p1, k1] twice, k1—27 (32, 37, 42, 47, 52) sts each side.
Dec row 2 (WS) Working both sides at once, dec 1 st at each neck edge. Rep last 2 rows 3 times more—17 (22, 27, 32, 37, 42) sts.
Rep dec row 1 every other row until 11 (10, 9, 8, 7, 6) sts rem. Rep dec row 2 every other row until 3 sts rem.
Bind off.

Strap

With smaller needles and B, cast on 44 (46, 46, 48, 48, 50) sts, pick up and knit 18 (22, 24, 26, 28, 30) sts from right front neckline, pm, k1 from holder, pm, pick up and knit 18 (22, 24, 26, 28, 30) sts from left front neckline, cast on 44 (46, 46, 48, 48, 50) sts—125 (137, 141, 149, 153, 161) sts. **Row 1 (WS)** Knit.
Row 2 (RS) Knit to 2 sts before marker, ssk, sl m, k1, sl m, k2tog, k to end.
Rep rows 1 and 2 twice more. Bind off.

FINISHING

Seam sides. Sew ends of straps to back at edges.

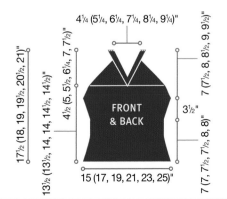

4¼ (5¼, 6¼, 7¼, 8¼, 9¼)"

17½ (18, 19, 19½, 20½, 21)"

13½ (13½, 14, 14, 14½, 14½)"

4½ (5, 5½, 6¼, 7, 7½)"

FRONT & BACK

3½"

7 (7½, 8, 8½, 9, 9½)"

7 (7, 7½, 7½, 8, 8)"

15 (17, 19, 21, 23, 25)"

SUMMER *floral top*

You'll Need

YARN 2

- 7oz/200g, 550yd/500m (7oz/200g, 550yd/500m; 8¾oz/250g, 680yd/625m; 10½oz/300g, 820yd/750m; 10½oz/300g, 820yd/750m; 12¼oz/350g, 950yd/875m) of any sport weight cotton in natural (MC)
- 1¾oz/50g, 140yd/125m in orange (A) and green (B)

NEEDLES
- One pair size 8 (5mm) needles *or size to obtain gauge.*

OTHER MATERIALS
- Size G/6 (4mm) crochet hook

SIZES

Sized for X-Small (Small, Medium, Large, X-Large, XX-Large). Shown in size X-Small.

KNITTED MEASUREMENTS

- **Bust** 30 (34, 38, 42, 46, 50)"/76 (86.5, 96.5, 106.5, 116.5, 127)cm
- **Length** 21 (21½, 22, 23, 23½, 24)"/53 (54.5, 56, 58.5, 60, 61)cm

GAUGE

20 sts and 24 rows to 4"/10cm over St st using size 8 (5mm) needles. *Take time to check gauge.*

NOTE

Gauge and needles size are larger than suggested for this yarn. Fabric is meant to be loose for a light and airy look and feel.

BACK

With 2 strands of yarn held tog and MC, cast on 75 (85, 95, 105, 115, 125) sts. Cut one strand and cont in St st with single strand until piece measures 5"/12.5 cm from beg. Dec 1 st each side on next row, then every 6th row twice more—69 (79, 89, 99, 109, 119) sts. Work even until piece measures 9½ (9½, 9½, 10, 10, 10)"/24 (24, 24, 25.5, 25.5, 25.5)cm from beg. Inc 1 st each side on next row, then every 6th row twice more—75 (85, 95, 105, 115, 125) sts. Work even until piece measures 14 (14, 14, 14½, 14½, 14½)"/35.5 (35.5, 35.5, 37, 37, 37)cm from beg.

Shape armhole

Bind off 4 (5, 5, 6, 6, 7) sts at beg of next 2 rows, 2 sts at beg of next 2 (4, 6, 6, 8, 10) rows. Dec 1 st each side every other row 3 (3, 4, 5, 7, 8) times. Work even on rem 57 (61, 65, 71, 73, 75) sts until armhole measures 6 (6½, 7, 7½, 8, 8½)"/15 (16.5, 18, 19, 20.5, 21.5)cm.

Shape neck

Next row (RS) Work 13 (14, 16, 19, 19, 20) sts, join 2nd ball of yarn and bind off center 31 (33, 33, 33, 35, 35) sts, work to end. Working both sides at once, bind off from each neck edge 2 sts once, 1 st once. Bind off rem 10 (11, 13, 16, 16, 17) sts each side for shoulders.

FRONT

Work as for back until armhole measures ½ (1, 1, 1½, 1½, 2)"/1.5 (2.5, 2.5, 4, 4, 5) cm.

Shape neck

Cont armhole shaping, bind off center st and working both sides at once, dec 1

st at each neck edge (1 st in from edge) every other row 18 (19, 19, 19, 20, 20) times. Work even until same length as back. Bind off rem 10 (11, 13, 16, 16, 17) sts each side for shoulders.

FINISHING

Block pieces lightly to measurements. Sew one shoulder seam.

Neck edging

With RS facing, pick up and k 1 st in each st and row around neck edge. Bind off knitwise. Sew 2nd shoulder seam.

Armhole edging

Work same as neck edging. Sew side seams, leaving 5"/12.5cm from lower edge unsewn for side slits. Work edging around slits same as neck edging.

Flowers and leaves

With crochet hook and A and B, work various sizes of flowers and leaves and sew to front (see photo for placement). For instructions, please visit: www.go-crafty.com.

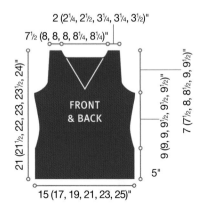

Rose Callahan

SCOOP neck tank

You'll Need

YARN

- 7oz/200g, 450yd/400m (8¾oz/250g, 560yd/505m; 10½oz/300g, 675yd/610m; 12¼oz/350g, 785yd/720m; 14oz/400g, 900yd/820m; 14oz/400g, 900yd/820m) of any DK weight cotton blend.

NEEDLES

- One pair size 8 (5mm) knitting needles *or size to obtain gauge.*
- One size 8 (5mm) circular needle, 16"/40cm long

SIZES

Sized for X-Small (Small, Medium, Large, 1-X, 2-X). Shown in size X-Small.

KNITTED MEASUREMENTS

- **Bust** 29½ (33½, 37½, 42½, 45½, 50½)"/75 (85, 95, 108, 115.5, 128)cm
- **Length** 20½ (21, 21½, 22, 22½, 23)"/52 (53.5, 54.5, 56, 57, 58.5)cm

GAUGE

20 sts and 38 rows to 4"/10cm over St st using size 8 (5mm) needles.
Take time to check gauge.

BACK

Cast on 74 (84, 94, 106, 114, 126) sts. Work in k2, p2 rib for ¾"/2cm. Change to St st and work even until piece measures 5"/13cm from beg, ending with a WS row.

Beg rib pat

Next row (RS) [K2, p2] 6 times, k 26 (36, 46, 58, 66, 78), [p2, k2] 6 times. Work in rib pat as established until piece measures 9"/23cm from beg. Cont to work all sts in St st until piece measures 13"/33cm from beg.

Shape armhole

Bind off 3 (3, 3, 5, 6, 8) sts at beg of next 2 rows. Dec 1 st each side every other row 4 (4, 5, 6, 8, 10) times, then every 4th row 3 (7, 8, 9, 9, 10) times—54 (56, 62, 66, 68, 70) sts. Work even until armhole measures 5½ (6, 6½, 7, 7½, 8)"/14 (15, 16.5, 18, 19, 20.5)cm, ending with a WS row.

Shape neck

Next (RS) row K16 (16, 17, 17, 18, 18), join a 2nd ball of yarn and bind off center 22 (24, 28, 32, 32, 34) sts, k to end. Working both sides at once, dec 1 st from each neck edge every row 9 (9, 10, 10, 11, 11) times, then every other row twice—5 sts. Work even until armhole measures 7½ (8, 8½, 9, 9½, 10)"/19 (20.5, 21.5, 23, 24, 25.5)cm. Bind off.

FRONT

Work as for back until armhole measures 1 (1½, 2, 2½, 3, 3½)"/2.5 (4, 5, 6.5, 7.5, 9)cm, ending with a WS row. Cont to work armhole shaping, AT THE SAME TIME work neck shaping as foll:

Next row (RS) Knit to center 16 (18, 20, 22, 24, 26) sts, join 2nd ball of yarn, bind off center 16 (18, 20, 22, 24, 26) sts, knit to end. Working both sides at once, dec 1 st at each neck edge every row 6 (6, 7, 7, 7, 7) times, then every other row 8 (8, 9, 10, 10, 10) times—5 sts. Work evenly until armhole measures same as for back, bind off.

FINISHING

Sew shoulder and side seams.

Neckband

With RS facing and circular needle, pick up and k 100 (104, 112, 120, 124, 128) sts evenly around neck edge. Join and work in k2, p2 rib for ¾"/2cm. Bind off in rib.

Armhole bands

With RS facing and circular needle, pick up and k 76 (80, 84, 88, 92, 96) sts evenly around armhole edge. Join and work in k2, p2 rib for ¾"/2cm. Bind off in rib.

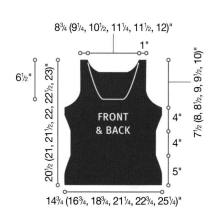

8¾ (9¼, 10½, 11¼, 11½, 12)"

1"

6½"

7½ (8, 8½, 9, 9½, 10)"

FRONT & BACK

4"

4"

5"

20½ (21, 21½, 22, 22½, 23)"

14¾ (16¾, 18¾, 21¼, 22¾, 25¼)"

Ross Callahan

BOAT neck tank

You'll Need

YARN (3)

- 10½oz/300g, 690yd/630m (12¼oz/350g, 805yd/740m; 14oz/400g, 920yd/840m; 15¾oz/450g, 1040yd/950m; 18oz/550g, 1150yd/1050m; 20oz/600g, 1270yd/1160m) of any DK weight cotton.

NEEDLES

- One pair each size 3 and 4 (3.25 and 3.5mm) needles *or size to obtain gauge.*

OTHER MATERIALS

- Two size 4 (3.5mm) double-pointed needles (dpns) for I-cord

SIZES

Sized for Small, Medium, Large, 1X, 2X, 3X. Shown in size Small.

KNITTED MEASUREMENTS

- **Bust** 32 (36, 40, 44, 48, 52)"/81 (91.5, 101.5, 111.5, 122, 132)cm
- **Length** 21 (21½, 22, 22½, 23, 23½)"/53.5 (54.5, 56, 57, 58.5, 59.5)cm

GAUGE

24 sts and 34 rows to 4"/10cm over pat st using larger needles (after blocking). *Take time to check gauge.*

STITCH GLOSSARY

K4, p2 rib

(multiple of 6 sts plus 2)
Row 1 (RS) P1, *p2, k4; rep from *, end k1.
Row 2 P1, *p4, k2; rep from *, end k1.

Rep rows 1 and 2 for k4, p2 rib.

Pattern stitch

(multiple of 6 sts plus 2)
Row 1 (RS) P1, *p2, k4; rep from *, end k1.
Row 2 and all WS rows Knit the k sts and purl the p sts.
Row 3 P1, *p3, k3; rep from *, end k1.
Row 5 P1, *p4, k2; rep from *, end k1.
Row 7 K1, *k1, p4, k1; rep from *, end k1.
Row 9 K1, *k2, p3, k1; rep from *, end k1.
Row 11 K1, *k3, p2, k1; rep from *, end k1.
Row 12 Rep row 2.
Rep rows 1–12 for pat st.

BACK

With smaller needles, cast on 98 (110, 122, 134, 146, 158) sts. Work in k4, p2 rib for 6"/15cm, end with a WS row. Change to larger needles. Cont in pat st until piece measures 14"/35.5cm from beg, end with a WS row.

Shape armholes

Bind off 5 (6, 7, 8, 9, 10) sts at beg of next 2 rows, then 2 sts at beg of next 2 (2, 4, 4, 4, 4) rows—84 (94, 100, 110, 120) sts.
Next (dec) row (RS) K1, ssk, work to last 3 sts, k2tog, k1. Rep dec row every other row 4 (5, 5, 7, 9, 11) times more, then every 4th row 3 times—68 (76, 82, 88, 94, 100) sts. Work even until armhole measures 6½ (7, 7½, 8, 8½, 9)"/16.5 (17.5, 19, 20.5, 21.5, 23)cm, end with a WS row.

Shape neck

Next row (RS) Work across first 10 (14, 16, 19, 21, 24) sts, join a 2nd ball of yarn and bind off center 48 (48, 50, 50, 52, 52) sts, work to end.
Working both sides at once, bind off 2 sts from each neck edge once. Work even on 8 (12, 14, 17, 19, 22) sts each side until armhole measures 7 (7½, 8,

8½, 9, 9½)"/17.5 (19, 20.5, 21.5, 23, 24) cm, end with a WS row. Bind off each side for shoulders.

FRONT

Work same as back until armhole measures 5½ (6, 6½, 7, 7½, 8)"/14 (15, 16.5, 17.5, 19, 20.5)cm, end with a WS row.

Shape neck

Next row (RS) Work across first 23 (27, 29, 32, 34, 37) sts, join a 2nd ball of yarn and bind off center 22 (22, 24, 24, 26, 26) sts, work to end.
Working both sides at once, bind off 5 sts from each neck edge once, then 4 sts once, then 3 sts once, then 2 sts once, then 1 st once.
Work even on 8 (12, 14, 17, 19, 22) sts each side until piece measures same length as back to shoulder, end with a WS row. Bind off each side for shoulders.

FINISHING

Block pieces to measurements. Sew shoulder and side seams.

I-cord neck edging and ties

With RS of front neck facing, place a marker 1½"/4cm from side edge of right front neck (first neck marker), then place another marker 1"/2.5cm to the right of first marker (2nd neck marker).
For first tie, with dpn, cast on 3 sts

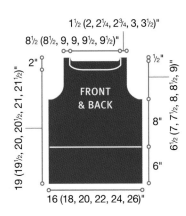

1½ (2, 2¼, 2¾, 3, 3½)"

8½ (8½, 9, 9, 9½, 9½)"

2"

½"

FRONT & BACK

8"

6½ (7, 7½, 8, 8½, 9)"

19 (19½, 20, 20½, 21, 21½)"

6"

16 (18, 20, 22, 24, 26)"

Rose Callahan

leaving a long tail. Work in I-cord as foll:

*Next row (RS) With 2nd dpn, k3, do not turn. Slide sts back to beg of needle to work next row from RS; rep from * until I-cord measures 4 (4, 4, 5, 5, 5)"/10 (10, 10, 12.5, 12.5, 12.5)cm from beg. Do not slide sts back to beg of needle. Apply I-cord to neck edge as foll: With WS of neck facing and working from right to left, beg at 2nd neck marker.

*Using dpn holding I-cord sts, pick up and k 1 st in neck edge. Slide sts back to beg of needle, k2, k2tog tbl, do not slide sts back to beg of needle; rep from * evenly spaced around neck edge to first neck marker.

For 2nd tie, cont in I-cord without attaching for 4 (4, 4, 5, 5, 5)"/10 (10, 10, 12.5, 12.5, 12.5)cm. Cut yarn, leaving a long tail.

Thread tail into tapestry needle, then weave needle through sts. Pull tail to gather; fasten off securely.

Rep for first tie.

Armhole edging

With dpn, cast on 3 sts. Do not slide sts back to beg of needle. Apply I-cord to armhole edge as foll: With WS of armhole facing and working from right to left, beg at side seam.

*Using dpns holding I-cord sts, pick up and k 1 st in armhole edge. Slide sts back to beg of needle, k2, k2tog tbl, do not slide sts back to beg of needle; rep from * evenly spaced around armhole edge. Cut yarn, leaving a long tail. Graft ends tog.

RUFFLE trim tank

You'll Need

YARN

- 14oz/400g, 720yd/660m (17½oz/500g, 900yd/825m; 21oz/600g, 1080yd/990m; 21oz/600g, 1080yd/990m) of any worsted weight cotton.

NEEDLES

- One pair each sizes 6 and 7 (4 and 4.5mm) needles *or size to obtain gauge.*

OTHER MATERIALS

- Three ⁷/₁₆-inch (11.5mm) buttons
- Stitch markers and stitch holders

SIZES

Sized for Small, Medium, Large, X-Large. Shown in size Small.

KNITTED MEASUREMENTS

- **Bust** 32 (34½, 37, 39½)"/81 (87.5, 94, 100)cm
- **Length** 23¼ (24, 24¾, 25½)"/59 (61, 63, 64.5)cm

GAUGE

19 sts and 25 rows to 4"/10cm over St st using larger needles.
Take time to check gauge.

BACK

With larger needles, cast on 116 (122, 128, 134) sts.

Row 1 (WS) Knit. **Row 2 (RS)** Knit.
Row 3 *K1, p1; rep from * to end.
Rows 4 and 5 K the purl sts and p the knit sts. **Rows 6 and 7** Knit.
Set-up row (RS) K20 (21, 22, 23), pm, [k19 (20, 21, 22), pm] 4 times, k20 (21, 22, 23).
Work even in St st for 7 rows more.
Dec row 1 (RS) *K to 2 sts before marker, p2tog, sl marker; rep from * 4 times more, k to end—5 sts dec'd. Work even in St st for 7 rows more.
Dec row 2 (RS) *K to marker, sl marker, p2tog; rep from * 4 times more, k to end—5 sts dec'd. Work even in St st for 7 rows more. Rep last 16 rows 3 times more—76 (82, 88, 94) sts.
Next row (RS) Purl (for ridge on the RS)**.
Piece measures approx 12½"/32cm from beg. Work even in St st until piece measures 3½(4, 4½, 5)"/9 (10, 11.5, 12.5)cm from the ridge, end with a RS row.
Beg armhole detail
+**Row 1 (WS)** K9 (9, 10, 11), p58 (64, 68, 72), k9 (9, 10, 11). **Row 2 (RS)** Knit.
Row 3 Rep row 1. **Row 4** Bind off 6 (6, 7, 8) sts firmly, work to end. **Row 5** Bind off 6 (6, 7, 8) sts firmly, k2, work to last 3 sts, k3. **Row 6** K2, SKP, work to last 4 sts, k2tog, k2. **Row 7** K3, work to last 3 sts, k3. Rep [rows 6 and 7] 2 (4, 4, 5) times more—58 (60, 64, 66) sts.
Next row (RS) Work even.+
Next row (WS) K3, work to last 3 sts, k3. Rep last 2 rows until armhole (measured from the first armhole bind-off) measures 3½ (3¾, 4, 4¼)"/9 (9.5, 10, 11)cm.
Begin strap detail
Note Be certain to work the center neck garter section *tightly* to keep the edge flat.
Row 1 (RS) K10, [k2tog, k4] 6 (6, 7, 7) times, k2tog, k0 (2, 0, 2), k10—51 (53, 56, 58) sts. **Row 2** K3, p4, k37 (39, 42, 44), p4, k3. **Row 3** *K2, k1, p1, k1, k2*, k37 (39, 42, 44); rep between *'s once.
Row 4 *P2, k1, p1, k1, p2*, k3, join a 2nd ball of yarn and bind off center 31 (33, 36, 38) sts, k2; rep between *'s once.

Change to smaller needles.
Next row (RS) *K2, k1, p1, k1, k2*, k1, k2tog; on 2nd strap, k2tog, k1; rep between *'s once. **Next row (WS)** *P2, k1, p1, k1, p2*, k2tog; on 2nd strap, k2tog; rep between *'s once.
Next row (RS) K2, k1, p1, k2, SKP; on 2nd strap, k2tog, k2, p1, k1, k2. There are 7 sts each side for the straps. Cont in established pat (that is, rep between *'s on rows 3 and 4) until armhole measures 6¾ (7, 7¼, 7½)"/17 (18, 18.5, 19)cm (measured from the first armhole bind-off). Leave sts on holders.

FRONT

Work as for back up to the purl ridge at **. Piece measures approx 12½"/32cm from beg.
Front bodice
Row 1 (WS) P34 (37, 40, 43), k1, p6, k1, p34 (37, 40, 43). **Row 2 (RS)** K34 (37, 40, 43), p1, k6, p1, k34 (37, 40, 43).
Rep last 2 rows until bodice measures 3½ (4, 4½, 5)"/9 (10, 11.5, 12.5)cm from the purl ridge.
Begin armhole detail
Work as for back between +'s, (only, cont with the center 8 sts as established).
Shape neck
Row 1 (WS) K3, p4, k44 (46, 50, 52), p4, k3.
Row 2 (RS) *K2, k1, p1, k1, k2*, k44 (46, 50, 52); rep between *'s once.

9¼ (9½, 10½, 11)" 1"
2¾"
4 (4¼, 4½, 4¾)"
23¼ (24, 24¾, 25½)"
FRONT & BACK
11½"
4 (4½, 5, 5½)"
1"
24½ (25½, 27, 28¼)"
16 (17¼, 18½, 19¾)"

Row 3 *P2, k1, p1, k1, p2*, k3, join a 2nd ball of yarn and bind off center 38 (40, 44, 46) sts, k2; rep between *'s once.

Row 4 *K2, k1, p1, k1, k2*, k1, k2tog; on 2nd strap, k2tog, k1; rep between *'s once. Change to smaller needles.

Next 2 rows Complete as for back straps. There are 7 sts each side. Work even until armhole measures same as back. Using 3-needle bind off method, join the straps tog.

Ruffle trim

To work the right front ruffle trim, using the purl st that runs along the right neck edge, with RS facing and smaller needles, beg at the top bodice edge, pick up and k 31 (33, 37, 39) sts on the purl ridge.

Row 1 (WS) [P1, p in front and back of next st] 15 (16, 18, 19) times, p1— 46 (49, 55, 58) sts. Knit 1 row. Purl 1 row. Bind off purlwise. To work the left front ruffle trim, beg at the lower bodice edge and work as for the right front trim.

FINISHING

Sew side seams. Fold the ruffle trims under at the ends and seam inside the garter lines of the top and lower bodice. Sew on buttons. Lightly steam the ruffle trims flat and the body of the tank (do not steam or block the straps or bodice edges).

Rose Callahan

COLLARED TANK

You'll Need

YARN

- 10½oz/300g, 650yd/600m (10½oz/300g, 650yd/600m; 12¼oz/350g, 760yd/700m; 14oz/400g, 870yd/800m) of any worsted weight cotton.

NEEDLES

- One pair size 6 (4mm) knitting needles *or size to obtain gauge.*

OTHER MATERIALS

- Stitch holders
- Stitch markers
- Cable needle (cn)
- Size E-4 (3.5mm) crochet hook

SIZES
Sized for X-Small (Small, Medium, Large). Shown in size Small.

KNITTED MEASUREMENTS
- **Bust** 32 (35, 37, 40)"/81 (89, 94, 101.5)cm
- **Length** 21½ (22, 22½, 23)"/54.5 (56, 57, 58.5)cm

GAUGE
20 sts and 28 rows to 4"/10cm over St st using size 6 (4mm) needles.
Take time to check gauge.

STITCH GLOSSARY
2-st LC Sl 1 st to cn and hold to *front*, k1, k1 from cn.

Left cable band (over 15 sts)
Row 1 (RS) [P2, 2-st LC] 3 times, p2, k1.

Row 2 P1, k2, [p2, k2] 3 times.
Rep rows 1 and 2 for left cable band.

Right cable band (over 15 sts)
Row 1 (RS) K1, p2, [2-st LC, p2] 3 times.
Row 2 [K2, p2] 3 times, k2, p1.
Rep rows 1 and 2 for right cable band.

BACK
Cast on 61 (67, 73, 81) sts. Knit next row.
Inc row (RS) K2, M1, k to last 2 sts, M1, k2.
Next row K2, p to last 2 sts, k2. Rep last 2 rows 9 times more—81 (87, 93, 101) sts. Cont in St st and work even for 8 rows.
Dec row (RS) K2, ssk, k to last 4 sts, k2tog, k2. Rep last row every 4th row 3 times more—73 (79, 85, 93) sts. Work even until piece measures 7"/17.5cm from beg, end with a WS row.
Inc row (RS) K2, M1, k to last 2 sts, M1, k2. Rep last row every 4th row 3 times more. Work even on 81 (87, 93, 101) sts until piece measures 14"/35.5cm from beg, end with a WS row.

Shape armhole
Bind off 4 (4, 5, 6) sts at beg of next 2 rows.
Dec row (RS) K2, ssk, k to last 4 sts, k2tog, k2. Purl next row. Rep last 2 rows 15 (16, 16, 17) times more—41 (45, 49, 53) sts. Work even until armhole measures 6 (6½, 7, 7½)"/15 (16.5, 17.5, 19)cm, end with a WS row.
Shape neck and shoulder
Next row (RS) K 14 (16, 18, 20), place center 13 sts on holder for back neck, join a 2nd skein of yarn, k to end. Working both sides at once, bind off from each neck edge 3 sts once, 2 sts once. Dec 1 st from each neck edge every other row once. Work even on 8 (10, 12, 14) sts each side until armhole measures 7½ (8, 8½, 9)"/19 (20.5, 21.5, 23)cm, end with a WS row. Bind off each side.

FRONT
Work as for back until piece measures 11 (11½, 12, 12½)"/28 (29, 30.5, 31.5)cm from beg, end with a WS row.

Shape left neck
Next row (RS) K33 (36, 39, 43) sts, pm, work row 1 of left cable band over center 15 sts, place rem 33 (36, 39, 43) sts on holder for right front.
Next row Work row 2 of left cable band over first 15 sts, work to end. Work next 2 rows even.
Dec row (RS) Work to 2 sts before marker, k2tog, work to end. Rep dec row every other row 7 times more, every 4th row twice. AT THE SAME TIME, when piece measures same length as back to armhole, end with a WS row.

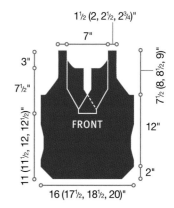

1½ (2, 2½, 2¾)"
7"
3"
7½"
FRONT
11 (11½, 12, 12½)"
7½ (8, 8½, 9)"
12"
2"
16 (17½, 18½, 20)"

1½ (2, 2½, 2¾)"
5"
1½"
BACK
20 (20½, 21, 21½)"

Rose Callahan

with a RS row.

Shape armhole

Next row (WS) Bind off 4 (4, 5, 6) sts.

Dec row (RS) Work as established to last 4 sts, k2tog, k2. Cont to work as for left front, reversing shaping.

FINISHING

Block pieces to measurements. Sew shoulder seams.

Collar

With RS facing, work row 1 of right cable band across 15 sts from right neck holder, pick up and k 15 sts along right front neck edge, 15 sts along right back neck edge, k 13 sts from back neck holder, pick up and k 15 sts along left back neck edge, 15 sts along left front neck edge, work row 1 of left cable band across 15 sts from left neck holder—103 sts.

Next row (WS) P1, *k2, p2; rep from *, end k2, p1.

Next row K1, p2, *2-st LC, p2; rep from *, end k1. Rep these 2 rows for 3"/7.5cm. Bind off. On WS, sew cast-on edge of right cable band to first row of left cable band. Sew side seams.

Bottom edging

With RS facing and crochet hook, join yarn with a sl st in right side seam.

Rnd 1 (RS) Ch 1, making sure that work lies flat, sc evenly around entire bottom edge, join rnd with a sl st in first sc. Fasten off.

Armhole edging

With RS facing and crochet hook, join yarn with a sl st in underarm seam. Rep rnd 1 as for bottom edging.

Neck edging

With RS facing and crochet hook, join yarn with a sl st in edge st at right cable band.

Rnd 1 (RS) Ch 1, sc evenly up front edge of right cable band. Fasten off. Rep on edge st at left cable band.

Shape armhole

Next row (RS) Bind off 4 (4, 5, 6) sts. Work 1 row even.

Dec row (RS) K2, ssk, work to end as established. Work next row even. Rep last 2 rows 10 (11, 11, 12) times more. When all shaping has been completed, work even on 23 (25, 27, 29) sts until armhole measures 4½ (5, 5½, 6)"/11.5 (12.5, 14, 15)cm, end with a WS row.

Next row (RS) Work across to last 7 sts, place these sts on holder. Work next row even.

Next row (RS) Work across to last 4 sts, place these sts on same holder. Work next row even. Rep last 2 rows once more. Work even on 8 (10, 12, 14) sts until piece measures same length as back to shoulder. Bind off.

Shape right neck

Cast 15 sts onto RH needle, pm, k sts from right front holder—48 (51, 54, 58) sts.

Next row (WS) Work to marker, work row 2 of right cable band over last 15 sts. Work next 2 rows even.

Dec row (RS) Work to marker, sl marker, ssk, work to end. Cont to work as for left neck, reversing shaping, AT THE SAME TIME, when piece measures same length as back to armhole, end

You'll Need

YARN

- 8¾oz/250g, 600yd/550m (10½oz/300g, 720yd/660m; 12¼oz/350g, 840yd/770m; 12¼oz/350g, 840yd/770m) of any worsted weight cotton/acrylic blend.

NEEDLES

- One pair size 8 (5mm) knitting needles *or size to obtain gauge.*

OTHER MATERIALS

- Stitch holders
- Stitch markers
- Cable needle (cn)

SIZES

Sized for X-Small (Small, Medium, Large). Shown in size X-Small.

KNITTED MEASUREMENTS

- **Bust** 30 (32, 35, 38)"/76 (81, 89, 96.5) cm
- **Width at bottom** 36 (38, 41, 44)"/91.5 (96.5, 104, 111.5)cm
- **Length** 24½ (25, 25½, 26)"/62 (63.5, 64.5, 66)cm

GAUGE

18 sts and 24 rows to 4"/10cm over St st.
Take time to check gauge.

NOTES

1 Back is made from the top edge to lower edge.
2 Front is made in one piece, from the ends of the straps down to lower front edge.

BACK

Beg at top back edge, cast on 68 (72, 78, 86) sts. Cont in St st and work even until piece measures 2"/5cm from beg, end with a WS row.

Shape sides

Inc row (RS) K2, M1, k to last 2 sts, M1, k2. Rep inc row every 12th row 7 times more—84 (88, 94, 102) sts. Work even until piece measures 18½"/47cm from beg. Bind off.

FRONT

Left strap

Cast on 18 (18, 20, 20) sts. Work cable pat as foll:
Rows 1, 3, 7, 9 and 11 (RS) K2, p2 (2, 3, 3), k10, p2 (2, 3, 3), k2.
Row 2 and all WS rows P2, k2 (2, 3, 3), p10, k2 (2, 3, 3), p2.
Row 5 K2, p2 (2, 3, 3), sl 5 sts to cn and hold to front, k5, k5 from cn, p2 (2, 3, 3), k2.
Rep rows 1–12 for left strap cable pat. Work even until piece measures 10 (11, 12, 13)"/25.5 (28, 30.5, 33) from beg, end with a WS. Place sts on holder.

Right strap

Cast on 18 (18, 20, 20) sts. Work cable pat as foll:
Rows 1, 3, 7, 9 and 11 (RS) K2, p2 (2, 3, 3), k10, p2 (2, 3, 3), k2.
Row 2 and all WS rows P2, k2 (2, 3, 3), p10, k2 (2, 3, 3), p2.
Row 5 K2, p2 (2, 3, 3), sl 5 sts to cn and hold to back, k5, k5 from cn, p2 (2, 3, 3), k2.
Rep rows 1–12 for right strap cable pat. Work even until piece measures same as left strap, end on same row (WS).
Next row (RS) Work across 18 (18, 20, 20) right strap sts, with same ball of yarn, cast on 30 sts, work across 18 (18, 20, 20) left strap sts—66 (66, 70, 70) sts.
Next row Work across 18 (18, 20, 20) left strap sts, k2, [p2, k2] 7 times, work

across 18 (18, 20, 20) right strap sts. Keeping 30 sts at center in k2, p2 rib and rem sts in cable pats as established, work even for 8 (6, 4, 2) rows.

Shape armhole

Inc row (RS) K2, M1, work to last 2 sts, M1, k2. Work one row even. Rep last 2 rows 1 (2, 3, 4) times more. Cast on 4 (5, 5, 8) sts at beg of next 2 rows—78 (82, 88, 96) sts.

Beg traveling cable pat

Set up row (RS) K6 (8, 9, 13), pm, k2, p2 (2, 3, 3), work right strap cable over 10 sts, p2 (2, 3, 3), work in rib across

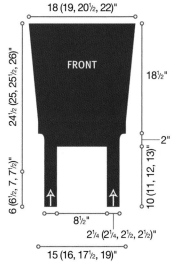

18 (19, 20½, 22)"

FRONT

18½"

24½ (25, 25½, 26)"

2"

6 (6½, 7, 7½)"

10 (11, 12, 13)"

8½"

2¼ (2¼, 2½, 2½)"

15 (16, 17½, 19)"

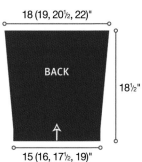

18 (19, 20½, 22)"

BACK

18½"

15 (16, 17½, 19)"

↑ Direction of work

next 17 sts, pm (center), work in rib across next 17 sts, p2 (2, 3, 3), work left strap cable over 10 sts, p2 (2, 3, 3), k2, pm, k6 (8, 9, 13). Work one row even.

Inc/dec row (RS) Work to first marker, M1, slip marker, work to 2 sts before next marker, k2tog, slip marker, ssk, work to next maker, slip marker, M1, work to end. Rep inc/dec row every 6th row 11 times more, AT THE SAME TIME, when piece measures 2"/5cm from cast-on edge of armhole, shape sides as for back. When all shaping is completed, work even on 94 (98, 104, 112) sts until piece measures same length as back to lower edge. Bind off.

FINISHING

Block pieces to measurements. Sew side seams. Sew ends of straps to top edge of back.

Rose Callahan

SLEEVELESS leaf top

You'll Need

YARN

- *Handicrafter Cotton* by Bernat, 1¾oz/50g balls, each approx 80yd/73m (cotton)
- 6 (7, 8, 9) balls #01 white

NEEDLES

- One pair each sizes 8 and 9 (5 and 5.5mm) needles *or size to obtain gauge.*
- Two size 8 (5mm) circular needles

OTHER MATERIALS

- Stitch markers

SIZES

Sized for Small (Medium, Large, X-Large). Shown in size Small.

KNITTED MEASUREMENTS

- **Bust** 34 (37, 40, 43)"/86.5 (94, 101.5, 109)cm
- **Length** 22 (22½, 23, 23½)"/56 (57, 58.5, 59.5)cm

GAUGE

13 sts to 3"/7.5cm and 24 rows to 4"/10cm over St st using smaller needles. One rose to 2¼"/5.5cm using larger needles.
Take time to check gauge.

STITCH GLOSSARY

Border pattern I
(multiple of 2 sts plus 1)
Row 1 (RS) Knit.
Rows 2 and 4 P1, *k1, p1; rep from * to end.
Row 3 K1, *p1, k1; rep from * to end.
Rows 5 and 6 Knit.

Work rows 1–6 for border pat I.

Border pattern II
(multiple of 2 sts plus 1)
Row 1 (WS) Knit.
Rows 2 and 4 K1, *p1, k1; rep from * to end.
Row 3 P1, *k1, p1; rep from * to end.
Row 5 Knit.
Work rows 1–5 for border pat II.

Leaf pattern
(worked over 11 sts)
Row 1 (RS) K3, k2tog, yo, k1, yo, ssk, k3.
Row 2 and all WS rows Purl.
Row 3 K2, k2tog, k1, yo, k1, yo, k1, ssk, k2.
Row 5 K1, k2tog, k2, yo, k1, yo, k2, ssk, k1.
Row 7 K2tog, k3, yo, k1, yo, k3, ssk.
Row 9 Yo, ssk, k7, k2tog, yo.
Row 11 K1, yo, ssk, k5, k2tog, yo, k1.
Row 13 K2, yo, ssk, k3, k2tog, yo, k2.
Row 15 K3, yo, ssk, k1, k2tog, yo, k3.
Row 17 K4, yo, SK2P, yo, k4.
Row 18 Purl.
Work rows 1–18 for leaf pat.

BACK

With smaller needles, cast on 75 (81, 87, 93) sts. Work rows 1–6 of border pat I. Cont in St st and work even until piece measures 3"/7.5cm from beg, end with a WS row.

Shape sides

Dec row (RS) K1, k2tog, k to last 3 sts, ssk, k1. Rep dec row every 6th row twice more—69 (75, 81, 87) sts. Work even until piece measures 10"/25.5cm from beg, end with a WS row.
Inc row (RS) K1, M1, k to last st, M1, k1. Rep inc row every 6th row twice more—75 (81, 87, 93) sts. Work even until piece measures 14"/35.5cm from beg, end with a WS row.

Shape armholes

Bind off 6 (6, 7, 7) sts at beg of next 2 rows, 3 sts at beg of next 2 rows—57 (63, 67, 73) sts.
Dec row (RS) K1, k2tog, k to last 3 sts, ssk, k1. Purl next row. Rep last 2 rows 2 (3, 3, 3) times more—51 (55, 59, 65) sts. Work even until armhole measures 7 (7½, 8, 8½)"/17.5 (19, 20.5, 21.5)cm, end with a WS row.

Shape shoulders and neck

Bind off 5 (6, 6, 8) sts at beg of next 2 rows, 5 (6, 7, 8) sts at beg of next 2 rows, AT THE SAME TIME, bind off center 25 (25, 27, 27) sts for neck, and working both sides at once, dec 1 st from each neck edge every row 3 times.

FRONT

Work as for back until border pat I is completed.
Next row (RS) K10 (12, 14, 16) sts, pm, k to end. Purl next row.

Beg first leaf pat

Row 1 (RS) K to marker, k 5, work leaf pat over next 11 sts, pm, k to end.
Row 2 P to marker, work leaf pat over next 11 sts, p to end. Cont to work as established to row 18, dropping second marker on last row. AT THE SAME TIME, when piece measures 3"/7.5cm from beg, shape sides as for back.

Beg second leaf pat

Row 1 (RS) K to marker, k 13, work leaf pat over next 11 sts, pm, k to end.
Row 2 P to marker, work leaf pat over next 11 sts, p to end. Cont to work as

Rose Callahan

Shape neck and shoulders

Next row (RS) K 16 (18, 19, 22) sts, join another ball of yarn and bind off center 19 (19, 21, 21) sts for front neck, k to end. Working both sides at once, bind off from each neck edge 2 sts twice, then dec 1 st every other row twice—10 (12, 13, 16) sts each side. Work even until piece measures same length as back to shoulders, end with a WS row. Shape shoulders as for back.

FINISHING

Block pieces to measurements. Sew shoulder seams. Locate and mark center st of bound-off sts of front neck.

Neckband

With RS facing and circular needle, pick up and k 85 (85, 89, 89) sts evenly spaced around neck edge beg at st to the left of marked center st and ending at st to the right of marked center st. Working back and forth using two circular needles, work rows 1–5 of border pat II. Bind off all sts loosely knitwise.

Armhole bands

With RS facing and smaller needles, pick up and k 79 (83, 89, 95) sts evenly spaced along armhole edge. Work rows 1–5 of border pat II. Bind off all sts knitwise. Sew side seams.

Roses (make 3)

With larger needles, cast on 11 sts. **Row 1** K1, [work (k1, p1) in next st] 9 times, k1—20 sts. **Row 2** Purl. **Row 3** *K1, yo; rep from *, end k1. **Row 4** Knit—39 sts. **Row 5** *K 5, insert right needle under horizontal thread between 2 sts of 2 rows below and pull up a loop, place loop on LH needle then k this loop making a tight stitch; rep from * end k4. Bind off all sts loosely knitwise. Cut yarn leaving a 10"/25.5cm tail. Roll one end around itself to form a rose, then tack layers at several points to secure. Sew on roses as shown.

established to row 18, dropping second marker on last row.

Beg third leaf pat

Row 1 (RS) K to marker, work leaf pat over next 11 sts, pm, k to end.
Row 2 P to marker, work leaf pat over next 11 sts, p to end. Cont to work as established to row 18, dropping both markers on last row. Cont in St st and work as for back until armhole measures 5 (5½, 6, 6½)"/12.5 (14, 15, 16.5)cm, end with a WS row.

DROP STITCH tank {EASY}

Nick Norwood

You'll Need

YARN
- *Incredible* by Lion Brand Yarn Co., 1¾oz/50g balls, each approx 110yd/100m (nylon) 6 (7, 8, 9, 10, 11) balls in #211 emerald isle

NEEDLES
- One pair size 10 (6mm) needles *or size to obtain gauge.*

SIZES
Sized for Small (Medium, Large, 1X, 2X, 3X). Shown in size Small.

KNITTED MEASUREMENTS
- **Bust** 34 (37, 40, 44, 48, 52)"/86.5 (94, 101.5, 111.5, 122, 132)cm
- **Length** 20 (20½, 21½, 23, 23½, 24½)"/50.5 (52, 55, 58.5, 60, 62.5)cm

GAUGE
18 sts and 24 rows to 4"/10cm over pat st using size 10 (6mm) needles.
Take time to check gauge.

STITCH GLOSSARY
Pattern stitch
Rows 1–4 Knit.
Row 5 (RS) *K1, yo twice; rep from *, end k1.
Row 6 Knit, dropping extra yo's.
Rep rows 1–6 for pat st.

BACK
Cast on 76 (83, 90, 99, 108, 117) sts. Work even in pat st until piece measures approx 12½ (12½, 13, 14, 14, 14½)"/31.5 (31.5, 33, 35.5, 35.5, 37)cm from beg, end with row 2 or 6.
Shape armholes
Bind off 5 (6, 6, 7, 8, 9) sts at beg of next

2 rows. Dec 1 st each side every other row 5 (5, 6, 7, 8, 9) times—56 (61, 66, 71, 76, 81) sts. Work even until armhole measures approx 5¾ (6¼, 6¾, 7¼, 7¾, 8¼)"/14.5 (16, 17.5, 18.5, 20, 21)cm, end with row 2 or 6.
Shape neck
Next row (RS) K 19 (20, 22, 24, 26, 29), join another ball of yarn and bind off center 18 (21, 22, 23, 24, 23) sts for back neck, k to end. Working both sides at once, dec 1 st at each neck edge every other row twice—17 (18, 20, 22, 24, 27) sts. Work even until armhole measures 7 (7½, 8, 8½, 9, 9½)"/17.5 (19, 20.5, 21.5, 23, 24)cm, end with row 2 or 6.
Shape shoulders
Cont in garter st only and bind off from each shoulder edge 6 (6, 7, 7, 8, 9) sts twice, then 5 (6, 6, 8, 8, 9) sts once.

FRONT
Work as for back until armhole measures 3½ (4, 4½, 5, 5½, 6)"/9 (10, 11.5, 12.5, 14, 15)cm, end with row 2 or 6.
Shape neck

Next row (RS) K 20 (21, 23, 25, 27, 30), join another ball of yarn and bind off center 16 (19, 20, 21, 22, 21) sts for back neck, k to end. Working both sides at once, dec 1 st at each neck edge every other row 3 times. Work even on 17 (18, 20, 22, 24, 27) sts each side until piece measures same length as back to shoulder. Shape shoulders as for back.

FINISHING
Lightly block pieces to measurements. Sew shoulder and side seams.

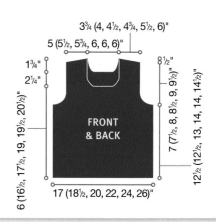

3¾ (4, 4½, 4¾, 5½, 6)"
5 (5½, 5¾, 6, 6, 6)"
1¾"
2¼"
½"
19½, 17½, 19, 19½, 20½)"
7 (7½, 8, 8½, 9, 9½)"
12½ (12½, 13, 14, 14, 14½)"
6 (16½, 17½, 19, 19½, 20½)"
17 (18½, 20, 22, 24, 26)"

FRONT & BACK